S. HRG. 104–101

NOMINATION OF JEFFREY M. LANG

HEARING

BEFORE THE

COMMITTEE ON FINANCE
UNITED STATES SENATE

ONE HUNDRED FOURTH CONGRESS

FIRST SESSION

ON THE

NOMINATION OF

JEFFREY M. LANG TO BE DEPUTY U.S. TRADE REPRESENTATIVE
WITH THE RANK OF AMBASSADOR

MAY 10, 1995

Printed for the use of the Committee on Finance

U.S. GOVERNMENT PRINTING OFFICE
92–695—CC WASHINGTON : 1995

For sale by the U.S. Government Printing Office
Superintendent of Documents, Congressional Sales Office, Washington, DC 20402
ISBN 0-16-047470-1

COMMITTEE ON FINANCE

BOB PACKWOOD, Oregon, *Chairman*

BOB DOLE, Kansas
WILLIAM V. ROTH, JR., Delaware
JOHN H. CHAFEE, Rhode Island
CHARLES E. GRASSLEY, Iowa
ORRIN G. HATCH, Utah
ALAN K. SIMPSON, Wyoming
LARRY PRESSLER, South Dakota
ALFONSE M. D'AMATO, New York
FRANK H. MURKOWSKI, Alaska
DON NICKLES, Oklahoma

DANIEL PATRICK MOYNIHAN, New York
MAX BAUCUS, Montana
BILL BRADLEY, New Jersey
DAVID PRYOR, Arkansas
JOHN D. ROCKEFELLER IV, West Virginia
JOHN BREAUX, Louisiana
KENT CONRAD, North Dakota
BOB GRAHAM, Florida
CAROL MOSELEY-BRAUN, Illinois

LINDY L. PAULL, *Staff Director and Chief Counsel*
LAWRENCE O'DONNELL, JR., *Minority Staff Director*

CONTENTS

OPENING STATEMENT

ADMINISTRATION NOMINEE

NOMINATION OF JEFFREY M. LANG TO BE DEPUTY U.S. TRADE REPRESENTATIVE

WEDNESDAY, MAY 10, 1995

U.S. SENATE,
COMMITTEE ON FINANCE,
Washington, DC.

The hearing was convened, pursuant to notice, at 11:19 a.m., in room SD–215, Dirksen Senate Office Building, Hon. Bob Packwood (chairman of the committee) presiding.

Also present: Senators Dole, Chafee, Grassley, Pressler, D'Amato, Murkowski, Nickles, Baucus, Bradley, and Graham.

Senator DOLE. Can I just say one word? I have to leave.

The CHAIRMAN. Absolutely. Go ahead.

Senator DOLE. I am for the nominee, so I do not want to screw anything up here with questions. But I would hope you could comment on the banana case. I know it may be brought up by others, but I hope to talk to Ambassador Kantor about it today, and if you have any comments for the record, they would be appreciated.

Mr. LANG. I should just say, Mr. Leader, that the ethics people tell me that I have to recuse myself from that matter.

Senator DOLE. Oh, really? All right. Well, do not comment on the banana case. [Laughter.]

OPENING STATEMENT OF HON. BOB PACKWOOD, A U.S. SENATOR FROM OREGON, CHAIRMAN, COMMITTEE ON FINANCE

The CHAIRMAN. I think we are ready. Mr. Lang, do you have anybody here to introduce before we start?

Mr. LANG. Yes, Mr. Chairman. Can I introduce my wife, Lynn, who is sitting behind me.

The CHAIRMAN. Lynn, good to have you with us. We are very familiar with your husband and have dealt with him for years and years, and find him a good fellow. Absent some skeleton that you might have to reveal about him——[Laughter]

The CHAIRMAN [continuing]. Why, I think he is probably going to be all right.

Mr. Lang.

STATEMENT OF JEFFREY M. LANG TO BE DEPUTY U.S. TRADE REPRESENTATIVE

Mr. LANG. Mr. Chairman, thank you. I have no prepared statement. I do not want to take a lot of your time. I just wanted to say, I appreciate very much your scheduling the hearing so quickly and I surrender myself to the committee for questions.

The CHAIRMAN. Do you have to recuse yourself on labor, environment, and trade?

Mr. LANG. They have not instructed me to do that. But, on any given matter, there is a review by the agency ethics officer before we proceed.

The CHAIRMAN. I do not mean a specific question, I just want to know your general views on the issue of tying labor and environment to trade.

Mr. LANG. Well, I think I ought to treat them separately.

The CHAIRMAN. All right.

Mr. LANG. On environment, we obviously have some environmental agreements out there with trade provisions in them and we have now trade agreements which have environmental provisions in them. So, as a practical matter, or as a legal matter, the two things have some relationship.

My judgment from private practice is that there is a lot of room for developing consensus about how these two fields of endeavor and American policy should relate to each other, and foreign countries are probably going to force us to do some of that, whether we want to or not. We now have the European Community threatening a sanction against American products in the fur industry.

The CHAIRMAN. In the what, fur?

Mr. LANG. Fur industry. Essentially on an environmental theory. So we are going to have to cope with this one way or another.

The CHAIRMAN. You said European countries.

Mr. LANG. Right.

The CHAIRMAN. Say that again.

Mr. LANG. Are threatening, in the future, to impose a sanction on American exports of fur. That is a problem for our producers.

The CHAIRMAN. Because we are violating their environmental standards, or what?

Mr. LANG. Essentially it is the way in which the fur is produced that is bothering them. That, of course, is one of the most difficult problems to address in the relationship between trade and environment. If the problem that bothers a domestic government about an import is something that happened to it before it ever went through the Customs filter, the nexus between the imported product and the alleged environmental offense is at the greatest remove from the trade process, yet we have examples of this going on.

Now, it seems to me that that is where this debate cuts. When are sanctions appropriate? I think that, insofar as possible, we have to avoid using trade sanctions on environmental matters, particularly when they are at that remove from the trade process.

But it also seems to me that there are going to be some circumstances in which we may want to do that, and what we really need on these subjects is the kind of discussion that you had in the Uruguay Round about these sanitary and phytosanitary measures, these health measures.

There, essentially, you worked out an agreement for dealing with these matters so that, for example, under that agreement a country can set its own risk level, the level of health risk it is willing to tolerate. But, if it imposes a sanction on imports it has to be on a national treatment basis and it has to be related on a scientific basis to the risk level they chose. Now, that is the kind of balancing that you can get through negotiation which you really do not achieve very well with a sanction system.

So, in the European case I cited, if they were to approach the American government about the problem and want to have a discussion about the standards for producing fur, that would be a useful discussion for us to engage in, but the sanction approach is not the way for them to proceed. That is basically my view on the subject. A lot of gray; a difficult area.

The CHAIRMAN. Let me come at this a different way, and you can separate labor and environment if you want.

I do not know what the administration ultimately will do, but we may or may not have another go at reenacting fast-track.

There is serious dispute as to whether or not environmental and labor issues should be included in fast-track. Do you have an opinion on that?

Mr. LANG. Yes. My opinion is that the President and Congress would both be well-served by having extension of fast-track, and it should be as broad as possible; as many countries, as many kinds of negotiations, and so on. There is a statutory mandate now to discuss labor in the WTO, there is a Trade and Environment Committee created at the Marrakesh Summit.

I do not know that you need to identify explicitly labor and environment in the legislation, but I certainly do not think it serves anyone's interests to exclude them, especially if we have to deal with problems like this fur issue. I would like to be able to discuss that problem and not have it excluded from our ability to discuss it.

The CHAIRMAN. All right. Another unrelated question then. At one time you supported a cross border environmental fee, or at least your writings did. Are you still of that mind?

Mr. LANG. Well, for one thing, I think what I said was that it ought to be given serious study. The problem I was trying to solve was the need to finance pollution control equipment in developing countries, which obviously costs a lot of money that some developing countries cannot raise.

I think that the negotiators in NAFTA came up with a better solution than that, which was the NADBank, the North American Development Bank, because that will provide that financing and it does not have the defect which the tax proposal had, which is, of course, that it is an increase in duties.

The CHAIRMAN. Senator Pressler, do you have any questions?

Senator PRESSLER. Yes. Yes, I do. I want to pursue just a few subjects in general.

Mr. LANG. Yes, sir.

Senator PRESSLER. First of all, let me welcome you here.

Mr. LANG. Thank you very much.

Senator PRESSLER. I am glad to see a fellow Army veteran. I think you are I are the only two guys around in government our age who served in the Army.

How did you happen to serve in the Army?

Mr. LANG. I was ROTC in college and signed up.

Senator PRESSLER. All right. Good for you. Well, I congratulate you.

Mr. LANG. Thank you.

Senator PRESSLER. I was merely a lieutenant; you are a captain. You say, "then captain." What does that mean?

Mr. LANG. I was a captain after I was a lieutenant, is what that means.

Senator PRESSLER. All right. Well, they never promoted me that high. All right.

Now, let me ask you some questions about agriculture, if I may, just in general, to see what your views are. You know, we have a problem up in South Dakota with the Canadian wheat, hogs, and timber coming in. The Canadians have a State Wheat Board. Free enterprise is competing and they under-price, and so on, and so forth.

What is your view of that?

Mr. LANG. Well, I think it is a state trading agency and that means that there is not the kind of open market for grains in Canada that we have tried to produce under the various farm bills here in the United States. It seems to me that is bound to result in distortions in price.

I am not familiar with the specific case. I know that there have been discussions about it over the last year. I think there is now a binational commission studying this matter, and hopefully they will report back to the Canadian officials and American officials with some kind of resolution of the problem. It seems to me that it is not going to produce an open market price if you have a state trading agency dealing in wheat.

Senator PRESSLER. Yes. The Canadians seem very hard to deal with. They seem to have a chip on their shoulder. I like Canada very much, but they seem to have a chip on their shoulder. Somehow, the White House has to be aggressive in dealing with them; the country music decision, the agricultural things, and the fishing disputes that my friends from Alaska have told me about.

What is with Canada, in your judgment?

Mr. LANG. Well, I do not know that I can characterize them in any particular way. I think they are good, tough negotiators. They have been a this a long time. They do not change their people over maybe as much as we do. You are right, you have to stick to your guns on these things and quietly but firmly maintain the American position. I do not have any problem with that. I do not know that I can characterize Canadians. They are tough negotiators.

Senator PRESSLER. All right. But I hope that we are equally tough, especially in agricultural trade, because it is hurting my farmers and small businessmen, and timber interests in western South Dakota and elsewhere.

Mr. LANG. Absolutely.

Senator PRESSLER. It is a two-way street, this thing. So that would be a message from me, and I think I have your commitment that you will carry that forward.

Let me ask you about this. Japan has a 50-percent tax on the import of U.S. meat; Korea has about a 60-percent tax on the import of U.S. meat. We do not have that sort of tax on the import of their products here. How can this be; how much longer will this go on?

Mr. LANG. Well, I have not looked at that specific sector as it came out of the Uruguay Round, except to know that we did have to repeal the Meat Import Act, I think, in connection with the Round, which probably adjusted our import regime substantially. But all I can do is look at the situation.

The one thing I can say about Korea is, in addition to those extraordinarily high rates of duty, they also have a lot of non-tariff barriers, in particular, shelf-life restrictions. My understanding is that USTR has identified that as a trade barrier, it has raised that in dispute settlement, and has begun the process that will lead to a WTO case on that matter. I support that.

Senator PRESSLER. All right. Well, that would mean a lot because cattle numbers are up in the country, hog numbers are up, broiler numbers are up. We are facing soft livestock prices for the next three or 4 years, I think. It is hard for me to explain to my ranchers who do not want any Federal aid, they just want a fair shake in international trade and they are not getting it over there.

What will you do in your job to help us out?

Mr. LANG. Well, I will do everything I can, just stay in close touch with you. I am not sure. Probably the lines of control between the two deputies will vary a little bit, but I will be involved in agriculture and I will look at this problem as soon as I get back downtown and become more familiar with it, and try to be helpful in every way I can.

Senator PRESSLER. Let me ask you a little bit about your philosophy with a specific example. It is generally assumed nowadays by economists that free trade is the best deal, that if we take away all barriers everybody will be better off. But I happen to have just bought a Harley-Davidson motorcycle last week. I am not going to join Hell's Angels, or anything like that. But I got the story of Harley-Davidson.

Mr. LANG. Terrific story.

Senator PRESSLER. In the 1970's it was about to go bankrupt and we barred the import, or stalled the import, of Japanese bikes for a few years and the Harley-Davidson now is so successful that it is hard to buy a Harley-Davidson. I bought this one in South Dakota and intend to ride it around my farm, and spy on my neighbors, and so forth, in disguise, to see what is going on.

But the point is, now there is a waiting list to buy Harley-Davidsons. They want them all over the world. Here is an example of where we used protectionism to protect one of our industries and it bounced back. This is contrary to all of the free trade theories, is it not?

Mr. LANG. No, I do not think it is, and I do not have a problem with it. That was actually an escape clause case, a safeguard case, that was brought in the early 1980's. I remember it very well.

In fact, I have a friend who used to work for this committee and he moved to London. He had two motorcycles, a Yamaha and a Harley, and he was told not to take the Harley because it would be stolen; everybody wanted a Harley.

I think that was an example of a good use of the safeguard clause for this reason. When the import protection was imposed, the company made a lot of commitments about restructuring itself, both financially and physically. It went through the kind of major overhaul of its business that we are always talking about American business having to do. So that period of temporary protection was used constructively to increase the competitiveness of that company. That is what the escape clause is for.

In fact, today if we take escape clause actions, the new World Trade Organization agreement has an important provision on this subject, which is that the first three years of the protection are without compensation to the adversely affected country, whereas, in the past, we could only take an escape clause action if we compensated the country that was adversely affected. So that is something that is new. We do not know how it will work.

But all through the 1980's when I worked on the staff of the committee, Senators were struggling with this effort to promote what is called positive adjustment in escape clause situations. I do not have any reservations about using the escape clause in an appropriate case. Obviously you have to prove serious injury as a result of imports to the International Trade Commission, and so on.

Senator PRESSLER. So, analogously, today if cattle prices collapse in the next year or two, would you be for doing what we did for Harley-Davidson, put a limit on imports or insist on certain things in Japan during a period of adjustment, as you say, and so forth? Could we use the Harley-Davidson example to——

Mr. LANG. Well, I do not think I would make a commitment about a specific case, but I think that they have the right under the law to go to the International Trade Commission and prove serious injury. We have just had an agricultural case come through that process and they should be free to use the law like everyone else, and if that is an affirmative result, I would evaluate the facts on their merits.

But what I am saying is, I do not have reservations about the theory of what you are talking about; I do not think it is inconsistent with free trade. It has been in the GATT from the beginning and is an important feature of American law. Frankly, it has not been used very much in recent years.

Senator PRESSLER. Yes. Well, what I am trying to say is, and I say to you as you go into your new job, that as a farm State Senator, I see these adjustments being made for our industrial sector, and I just thought of Harley-Davidson, whom I support very strongly and I own one now, if I can get it paid for, and I see them having had this protection in the 3-year period, and I see them prospering.

But everybody says to the farm sector, free trade is the best deal, ride the markets out, so on, and so forth. There seems to be a different set of principles applied to our agricultural trade than there is to our industrial trade. We do not tolerate 50-percent tariffs on industrial trade going into Japan, we do tolerate a 50-percent tax on beef going into Japan. A rancher in western South Dakota, from his point of view, that does not seem fair.

Mr. LANG. I understand.

Senator PRESSLER. Good.

Thank you, Mr. Chairman.

The CHAIRMAN. Thank you, Senator Pressler.

I have no other questions, Jeff.

[Whereupon, at 11:36 a.m., the hearing was concluded.]

APPENDIX

ADDITIONAL MATERIAL SUBMITTED

RESPONSES OF JEFFREY LANG TO QUESTIONS SUBMITTED BY SENATOR ROTH

1. It is my understanding that your main responsibilities will include agricultural trade matters, although you will share some of these issues with General Counsel and Ambassador-designate Ira Shapiro with respect to agricultural trade with Canada. What are your views on the trade barriers our poultry, dairy and egg producers face in gaining access to the Canadian market? Do you believe that our free trade agreement with Canada should mean eventual tariff-free trade for all goods, including agriculture?

A. Region-wide free trade for all goods, including agriculture, is a fundamental goal that all three NAFTA parties have endorsed. The central issue in the pending disagreement with Canada, as I understand it, is whether Canada is violating its NAFTA obligations by applying Uruguay Round-mandated "tariffied" duties to U.S. dairy, poultry and egg products. The United States believes that the application of Canada's higher tier tariffs to U.S. products is inconsistent with NAFTA provisions which prohibit the introduction of new duties between the parties. Canada, of course, disagrees. My review of this issue has convinced me that the U.S. position is well-founded.

2. On February 2, Ambassador Kantor formally requested consultations with the Canadian government regarding our concerns that Canada was in breach of its NAFTA tariff commitments on poultry, dairy and eggs. What specific progress, if any, has been made since then to resolve this very serious matter?

A. The requested consultations were held in Ottawa in March 1. That discussion helped clarify the positions of both sides, but produced no resolution.

3. It seems that the only way to address our trade concerns on poultry is to initiate formal NAFTA dispute settlement panel proceedings. Ambassador Kantor's request for consultations was the initial step to an actual arbitral panel process, and it is my understanding that the NAFTA Commission must meet before and arbitral panel can be established. Has the Commission met at all this year? Do you support this matter being placed on the agenda for the scheduled June Commission meeting, and if not, why not? Do you support the establishment of a NAFTA dispute settlement panel to address this issue?

A. The NAFTA Commission has not met this year. A meeting is tentatively being planned for early June. I understand that Ambassador Kantor is planning to request that Canada's dairy, poultry and egg tariffs be placed on the agenda for the upcoming meeting. If the Commission considers the issue and is unable to offer a solution acceptable to the Parties, then the Administration must decide whether to move to the next step in the NAFTA dispute settlement process -- a request for a dispute settlement panel. NAFTA rules require a 30-day minimum waiting period after the NAFTA Commission considers the matter before a panel request can be filed. Given the sensitivities surrounding this matter on both sides of the border, I expect that the Administration will continue to consult closely with the Congress and the affected private sector groups as this case proceeds.

4. I am concerned that our efforts to obtain free and fair access to the Canadian market for poultry will be met by Canadian complaints about our sugar and wheat restrictions. Can you assure me that the U.S. poultry industry won't be forced to accept less access to the Canadian market because of these trade restraints?

A. In bilateral negotiations on this issue, the U.S. position has been that the application by Canada of the higher-tier duties on poultry, dairy and egg products is inconsistent with Canada's NAFTA obligations and that these duties must be eliminated. Ambassador Kantor has indicated that we could have some flexibility with regard to a phase-out schedule, but Canada must commit to eliminate these duties over a specified time period. That seems to be a sound and reasonable position to me. I understand that USTR staff have been in frequent contact with representatives of the U.S. poultry industry on this matter. I can assure you that to the extent I am assigned to this matter, I will continue to consult with the interested producer groups and do everything in my power to accommodate their concerns.

JEFFREY M. LANG

Education:

B.A. Bowdoin College, 1964
LL.B. The University of Virginia Law School, 1967

Employment History:

Mar. '68–Mar. '70—U.S. Army: Lieutenant, then Captain.
Mar. '70–Dec. '75—Bridgeman, Long & Pyeatt: Associate.
Dec. '75–Nov. '79—U.S. International Trade Commission: Attorney, the Deputy General Counsel.
Nov. '79–Apr. '90—Senate Finance Committee: Professional staff member, then Chief International Trade Counsel.
Apr. '90–Feb. '95—Winthrop, Stimson, Putnam & Roberts: Counsel, then partner.

Professional Activities:

Vice Chairman, ABA International Trade Committee
Co-Chair, American Society of International Law Annual Meeting Committee for 1993–1994
Member, Virginia State Bar, District of Columbia Bar, Bar of the Court of International Trade, and the Court of Appeals for the Federal Circuit
Member, Rules Advisory Committee, Court of International Trade, 1980–81

Senate Finance Committee Questionnaire

Jeffrey M. Lang

A. BIOGRAPHICAL:

1. Name (Include any former names used)

   Jeffrey M. Lang

2. Address (List current residence address and mailing address)

   3026 Bennett Point Road
   P.O. Box 358
   Queenstown, MD 21658-0358

3. Date and place of birth

   June 23, 1942, Washington, DC

4. Marital Status (Include maiden name of wife or husband's name)

   Married, Lynn Zirkle (maiden)

5. Names and ages of children

   None

6. Education (List institution(s), dates attended, degree received and date degree granted)

   1960 to 1964
   Bowdoin College
   Brunswick, Maine 04011
   B.A., June 1964

   1964 to 1967
   The University of Virginia
   School of Law
   North Grounds
   Charlottesville, Virginia 22901
   L.L.B., June 1967

   Summer 1967
   International Court of Justice
   The Hague
   The Netherlands
   Certificate

7. Employment Records (List all positions held since college, including title or description of job, name of employer, location of work, and dates of inclusive employment)

   4/90 to 2/03/95
   Winthrop, Stimson, Putnam & Roberts
   1133 Connecticut Avenue, N.W.
   Washington, D.C. 20036
   Phone: 202-775-9800
   Positions Held: Counsel from 4/90 to 3/94
   Partner from 3/94 to 2/95

11/79 to 4/90
U.S. Senate Finance Committee
SD-205 Dirksen Senate Office Bldg.
Washington, D.C. 20510
Phone: 202-224-4515
Positions Held: Professional staff member from 11/79 to 1/87; Chief International Trade Counsel from 1/87 to 4/90.

12/75 to 11/79
U.S. International Trade Commission
500 E St., S.W.
Washington, D.C. 20436
Phone: 202-205-2000
Positions Held: Attorney Advisor from 12/75 to 2/78; Deputy General Counsel from 2/78 to 11/79

3/70 to 12/75
Bridgeman, Long & Pyeatt
(No Longer in Business)
Associate

3/68 to 3/70
United States Army
Rank: Lieutenant, then Captain

8. Government Experience (List any experiences in, or association with, Federal, State or local Governments including any advisory, consultative, honorary or part-time service or positions.

Please see the answer to A(7) above.

9. Memberships (List all memberships and offices held in professional, fraternal, scholarly, civic, charitable and other organizations).

I am an overseas member of the Reform Club in London, England. My wife and I are members of the Rodef Shalom Congregation in Falls Church, Virginia. My wife and I are members, and I have been since October 1994, a member of the Board of Directors of the Bennett Point Improvement Association, a civic association in the community where our principal residence is located. I am, and have been for over 20 years, a member of the State Bar of Virginia, the D.C. Bar, the D.C. Bar Association, and the American Society of International Law.

10. Political affiliations and activities (List all memberships and offices held in or financial contributions and services rendered to all political parties or election committee during the last ten years)

Beginning in 1992, I became a resident of Maryland, where I am a registered Democrat. Prior to 1992, I was a resident of Virginia where I had, on occasion, been active in Democratic Party politics since 1964. From 1979 to 1990, I worked on the Democratic Staff of the Committee on Finance, United States Senate.

11. Honors and Awards (List all scholarships, fellowships, honorary degrees, honorary society memberships, and any other special recognitions for outstanding service or achievement)

Vice Chairman (1992-93), ABA International Trade Committee. I was co-chair of the 1994 Annual Meeting of the American Society of International Law. I was one of two Americans who received a scholarship to attend The Hague Academy in 1967 (please see the question to question A(6), above).

12. Published Writings (List the titles, publishers and dates of books, articles, reports, or other published materials you have written)

March 1991: Co-author, "Identification and Assessment of Significant Open Issues in the TRIPs, TRIMs and Services GATT Negotiations," given at a one-day symposium on the Uruguay Round trade negotiations, sponsored by the ABA-U.S. Chamber of Commerce National Institute on the Uruguay Round, Washington, D.C. (Co-author: Charles S.Levy.)

February 1992: Essay, "The Operation of the 'Fast Track' Implementation Process As It May Affect A Possible North American Free Trade Agreement," published in The North American Free Trade Agreement: Issues, Options, Implications, on behalf of the International Trade Committee of the American Bar Association Section on International Law and Practice.

March 1993: Co-author, "North American - The Impact of NAFTA on Environmental Laws," published in the Latin American Law and Business Report, Volume 1, No. 4, pp. 21-24. (Co-authors: Paul Bousquet and Laura M. Brank.)

March 1993: "Trade and the Environment." Publication: Toward A New Trade Consensus, by the Economic Strategic Institute, Washington, D.C.

April 1993: Co-author, "NAFTA: Investment Provisions Provide Significant Protection to Investors," published in the Latin American Law and Business Report, Volume 1, No. 5, pp. 13-17. (Co-author: Laura M. Brank.)

May 1993: Co-author, "NAFTA Dispute Settlement Procedures," published in the Latin American Law and Business Report, Volume 1, No. 6, pp. 8-10. (Co-author: Laura M. Brank.)

May 1993: "Continuation of MFN Status for China?" American Conference Institute's Conference on "Doing Business in China and Hong Kong Into the Next Century."

July 1993: Co-author, "NAFTA: Procedures for the Elimination of Tariff and Non-Tariff Barriers," published in the Latin American Law and Business Report, Volume 1, No. 8, pp. 8-12. (Co-author: Michelle Gyles.)

August 1993: Co-author, "NAFTA: The Debates Continue. A Step in the Right Direction: Unlocking the Mexican Energy Market," published in the Latin American Law and Business Report, Volume 1, No. 9, pp. 12-16. (Co-author, Laura M. Brank.)

August 1993: Co-author, "Trade and the Environment," published in The Washington Quarterly, Volume 16:4, pp. 35-51. (Co-author: Kenneth Berlin.)

October 1993: Co-author, "NAFTA's Emergency Action Provisions: Potential Relief for Injured Industries," published in the Latin American Law and Business Report, Volume 1, No. 11, pp. 17-22. (Co-authors: Laura M. Brank and Rodolfo Fuentes.)

October 1993: Co-author, "EC Agreements With East/Central Europe Countries Offer Opportunities for U.S. and Non-EC Companies," published in the East/West Executive Guide, Volume 3, No. 10, pp. 9-10. (Co-author: Raymond S. Calamaro.)

December 1993: Co-author, "Determining Tariff Reduction Rates Under NAFTA," published in the U.S.-Mexico Free Trade Reporter, Volume 3, No. 11, 12/10/93. (Co-author: Michelle Gyles.)

January 1994: Co-author, "NAFTA and GATT--Ensuring a Peaceful Co-Existence," published in the U.S.-Mexico Free Trade Reporter, Volume 4, No. 2, 1/21/94. (Co-author: Michelle Gyles.)

April 1994: "Trade With India." American Conference Institute's Conference on "Doing Business With the New India."

May 1994: Co-author, "North American Development Bank Promises Millions to Environmental and Community Projects," published in the Latin American Law and Business Report, Volume 2, No. 5. (Co-authors: Laura M. Brank and Margaret K. Minister.)

July 1994: Co-author, "Handbook to the North American Free Trade Agreement," published by the WorldTrade Executive, Inc. (Co-authors: Christopher R. Wall, Stuart N. Brotman, Mark A. Monborne, Laura M. Brank and William L. Matthews.)

13. Speeches (Identify each speech which you have given during the past three years, the organization to which the speech was given, and supply two copies of each speech)

Please see Attachment No. 1

14. Qualifications (State what, in your opinion, qualifies you to serve in the particular position to which you have been nominated)

I am qualified for the position of Deputy U.S. Trade Representative by experience.

I have about 15 years of government experience in trade. As the Deputy General Counsel of the U.S. International Trade Commission in the late 1970's, I not only became familiar with the antidumping and other trade laws of the United States, but I also directed a major study for the Senate Finance Committee on the provisions of the agreements negotiated in the Tokyo Round of Multilateral Trade Negotiations. I have thus worked directly with tariff and non-tariff trade negotiations since at least 1978. My work at the USITC also involved considerable management responsibility.

My experience during nearly 11 years on the staff of the Senate Finance Committee brought me into contact with the problems of implementing the Tokyo Round agreements and with the trade enactments of the Congress in the 1980's, including the U.S.-China trade agreement implementing legislation in 1980; the Trade Act of 1984; the U.S.-Israel Free Trade Agreement implementing legislation in 1985; the U.S.-Canada Free Trade implementing legislation in 1988; and the Omnibus Trade Act of 1988. I traveled to Geneva and other destinations on the Committee's business during this period, and established relationships with foreign officials, which in some cases still endure. During this period, I operated under the supervision of Senators who, though Democrats, instructed me to operate as a service to Senators of both political parties, which gave me experience in the values of bipartisanship in American trade policy.

I believe that my experience in private life is also relevant to the question of my qualifications to be Deputy U.S. Trade Representative.

When I went to law school in the mid-1960's, curricula were not as generous in courses on the subject of trade as they are now, but I was able to take what courses were available at the University of Virginia law School from Dean Hardy Dillard (later appointed a judge of the International Court of Justice) and Monroe Leigh (later appointed Legal Adviser of the U.S. Department of State). These courses at least indicate an early interest in the subject matter.

In private practice, and particularly in my practice since leaving the staff of the Senate Finance Committee in 1990, I believe I acquired two types of qualifications. First, since much of my practice involved advising and representing U.S. companies in their trade problems outside the United States (particularly in Europe) and advising them with respect to trade negotiations, I have a reasonably current knowledge of the problems in trade today. For example, for the MTN Coalition (a coalition of U.S. companies interested in ambitious results in the Uruguay Round), I provided analysis of the negotiation from late 1990 until late 1993 (when the coalition disbanded).

Private practice also qualifies me in a more general way, in that it gave me insights into the impact of trade negotiations on private companies and other non-governmental organizations. For example, my private experience introduced me to the impressive efficiencies American business has undertaken recently, which is a factor in their being able to take advantage of the economic opportunities provided by American trade law and policy.

Finally, the very practice of law itself is, today, a business. The discipline of having to be efficient, to add value and to compete for clients is, in its own way, a qualification that would help me if confirmed.

C. FUTURE EMPLOYMENT RELATIONSHIPS

1. Will you sever all connections with your present employer, business firm, association or organization if you are confirmed by the Senate?

Yes

2. Do you have any plans after completing Government service to resume employment, affiliation or practice with your previous employer, business firm, association or organization?

No

3. Has anyone made a commitment to employ your services in any capacity after you leave Government service?

No

4. If confirmed, will you serve your full term of office?

Yes

D. POTENTIAL CONFLICTS OF INTEREST

1. Describe all financial arrangements, deferred compensation agreements, and other continuing dealings with business associates, clients, or customers.

As described in detail in response to question B.3., above, I will receive certain payments from the law firm in which I have recently been a partner. There are no other financial arrangements of any kind responsive to this question.

2. Indicate any investments, obligations, liabilities or other relationships which could involve potential conflicts of interest in the position to which you have been nominated.

I am not aware of any investment which could involve such a conflict, since our investments are in widely-held mutual funds, government securities, and so forth. Similarly, our only obligations or liabilities are the repayment of mortgages on our residences. These mortgages are held by corporate entities that present no appearance of conflict.

My wife and I do hold a mortgage in which the debtors are Lawrence and Daveylee Walders, two individuals. Mr Walders is a lawyer in Washington who may in the future be involved in matters that would come before the Office of the U.S. Trade Representative. In this regard, please see the response to question D.5, below.

3. Describe any business relationship, dealing or financial transaction which you have had during the last ten years, whether for yourself, on behalf of a client, or acting as an agent, that could in any way constitute or result in a possible conflict of interest in the position to which you have been nominated.

There are no such transactions prior to April 15, 1990, the date I entered into private law practice at the law firm of Winthrop, Stimson, Putnam & Roberts. Prior to the date during the ten year period identified in the question, I served on the staff of the Senate Committee on Finance and engaged in no such transactions.

Transactions that might fall within the scope of this question are listed in Attachment No. 4, which is a copy of Section D of the Executive Branch Public Financial Disclosure Report. This section required me to disclose sources of more than $5,000 in compensation received by me or my law firm for services provided directly by me during the period specified above.

4. Describe any activity during the past ten years in which you have been engaged for the purpose of directly or indirectly influencing or affecting the administration and execution of law of public policy.

   I assume that this question is limited to affecting the administration and execution of law or public policy in the United States. Prior to April 15, 1990, the date I commenced private law practice at Winthrop, Stimson, Putnam & Roberts, during the period covered by the question, I served on the staff of the Senate Finance Committee, and I assume that for purposes of this question, my activities in that job are not covered by this question. I engaged in no other such activities during the period before April 15, 1990 and within the reporting period.

   Subsequent to April 15, 1990, some or all of the activities listed in confidential Attachment No. 5, all of them connected with my law practice, may fall within the ambit of the request.

5. Explain how you will resolve any potential conflict of interest including any that may be disclosed by your responses to the above items. (Please provide a copy of any trust or other agreements.)

   I propose to recuse myself from matters reported in Part D of the Executive Branch Public Financial Disclosure Report and from any other matter that might be, or might create the appearance of a conflict of interest. While my wife and I maintain a joint revocable trust, there is no trust or other agreement establish to insulate me from our financial affairs, which involve only widely traded mutual funds, government securities, and other investments which do not create conflicts of interest in the position to which I am to be nominated. We do not plan significantly to alter these investments during my tenure in federal service, if confirmed.

6. Written opinions should be provided directly to the Committee by the General Counsel of the Agency to which you have been nominated and by the Director, Office of Government Ethics, Office of Personnel Management concerning potential conflicts of interest or any other legal barriers to your serving in this position.

   I have asked the agency ethics officer to provide these reports to the Committee.

E. TESTIFYING BEFORE CONGRESS

1. Are you willing to appear and testify before any duly constituted committee of the Congress on such occasions as you may be reasonably requested to do so?

   Yes

2. Are you willing to provide such information as is requested by such committee?

   Yes

F. OTHER

1. Provide the full details of any civil or criminal proceeding in which you were a defendant or any inquiry or investigation by the Federal, State or local agency in which you were the subject of the inquiry or investigation.

   There are none.

2. Give the full details of any proceeding, inquiry or investigation in which you were the subject of the proceeding, inquiry or investigation.

   Please see the answer to No. F(1) above.

3. Have you ever been convicted (including pleas of guilty or nolo contendere) of any criminal violation other than a minor traffic offense?

   No

4. Please advise the Committee of any additional information, favorable or unfavorable, which you feel should be considered in connection with your nomination.

   There is no additional information that I am aware of relevant to this nomination.

(Signature)

24 Feb 95

(Date)